Jenna's Pet

Claudia Moore
Illustrated by Jacqui Grantford

"I wish we had a pet," said Jenna.

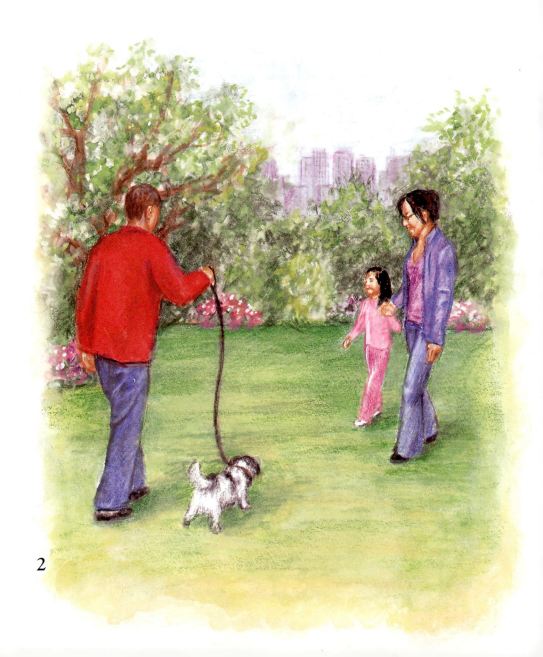

Mom smiled and said,
"Maybe we could have a squirrel."

"Squirrels have sharp claws.
They can climb," said Jenna.

"I don't think we can have a squirrel in our apartment."

"Maybe we could have an elephant,"
laughed Mom.

"Elephants have long trunks.
They carry things," said Jenna.
"I don't think we can have an elephant
in our apartment."

Mom smiled and said,
"Maybe we could have a seal."

"Seals have flippers.
They can swim," said Jenna.
"I don't think we can have a seal
in our apartment."

"Maybe we could have a cheetah,"
said Mom.

"Cheetahs have strong legs.
They can run fast," said Jenna.
"I don't think we can have a cheetah
in our apartment."

"Maybe we could have a kangaroo,"
laughed Mom.

"Kangaroos have long feet.
They can hop," said Jenna.
"I don't think we can have a kangaroo
in our apartment."

"What kind of pet would you like to have?" asked Mom.

"Let's get a fish!" said Jenna.

"Yes," said Mom.

"We can have a fish in our apartment!"